CW01511899

# THE POCKET

# DIOR

Published in 2025
by Gemini Gift Books
Part of Gemini Books Group

Based in Woodbridge and London

Marine House, Tide Mill Way,
Woodbridge, Suffolk IP12 1AP
United Kingdom

www.geminibooks.com

Text and Design © 2025 Gemini Gift Books Ltd
Part of the Gemini Pockets series

Text by Caroline Young
Cover illustration by Caroline Andrieu

ISBN 978-1-80247-321-6

Manufacturer's EU Representative: Eurolink Compliance Limited, 25 Herbert
Place, Dublin, D02 AY86, Republic of Ireland. admin@eurolink-europe.ie

Printed in Poland

10 9 8 7 6 5 4 3 2 1

MIX
Paper | Supporting
responsible forestry
FSC® C018236

**Picture Credits:** Alamy Stock Photo: Associated Press p53; Everett Collection Inc
p94; GRANGER - Historical Picture Archive p8; Grzegorz Czapski p87; Keystone
Press p112; Patti McConville p72; Retro AdArchives p4; Sueddeutsche Zeitung Photo
p27; WENN Rights Ltd p40. Getty Images: Christopher Polk p119.

# THE POCKET

# DIOR

DIOR

# CONTENTS

# INTRODUCTION

From the launch of his first collection in 1947, Christian Dior sent shock waves through fashion, pushing boundaries and reviving the art of couture. Dior's "New Look" helped Paris reclaim its spot as the fashion capital of the world, and was a welcome revival following the devastation of the Second World War. Faithful to dressmaking traditions, Dior's exquisite, feminine couture was a hit with stars including Marlene Dietrich and Elizabeth Taylor.

After Dior's sudden death in 1957, the fashion house hired a series of creative directors who reinvented and stayed true to its founder's beliefs. Yves Saint Laurent, Marc Bohan, Gianfranco Ferré, John Galliano, Raf Simons and Maria Grazia Chiuri have all pushed boundaries while reinterpreting the classics, like the iconic Bar suit. Through its visionary designs and redefinition of elegance, Dior's legacy has shaped the modern era of haute couture today.

"Women have instinctively understood that I dream of making them not only more beautiful, but also happier. That is why they have rewarded me with their patronage."

CHRISTIAN DIOR,
*DIOR BY DIOR* (1956)

# CHAPTER ONE

# HISTORY & HERITAGE

# IN THE BEGINNING

Christian Dior was born on 21 January 1905 in the Normandy town of Granville to a wealthy manufacturing family. He was the second eldest of Maurice and Madeleine Dior's five children, with brothers and sisters Raymond, Jacqueline, Bernard and Catherine. Granville is situated on a rocky peninsula overlooking the English Channel, and with its sweeping beaches and casinos, was known as the "Monaco of the North" over the summer months.

As Maurice's fertilizer business thrived, the family moved into a beautiful three-storey home, when Christian was still a baby. Known as "Les Rhumbs", it was situated on top of a windswept cliff, with views over the coastline to the Channel Islands.

# FAIRYTALE HOUSE

Dior was heavily influenced by the architecture and environment of Granville. The outside of the house was painted pale pink and grey, inspiring his signature colours. His beloved mother, Madeleine, adored fashion, and he would think back to the stylish dresses she wore around the house as he considered his own designs. The Japanese décor gave him a taste for silks embroidered with flowers. But his favourite room was the linen room, where the housemaids and seamstresses entertained him with fairytales.

# GRANVILLE GARDEN

As a boy, Christian loved to spend time in the garden at Granville, protected from the wind by a low stone wall. His mother took great pride in her English-style garden with its rose trellises. He loved the flowers so much that he would pore over botanical books to learn the names and descriptions.

The memories would stay with him, as the shape of the petals would inspire his early collections. The sweet scent of roses, gardenias and irises would be the basis of his signature perfume, Miss Dior, and he recreated the lily-of-the-valley in embroidery. He also named his Spring/Summer 1954 collection after his "lucky" flower.

"My whole way of life was influenced by its architecture and environment."

CHRISTIAN DIOR ON GRANVILLE,
*DIOR BY DIOR* (1956)

## BELLE ÉPOQUE

Christian's parents moved to Paris when
he was five, keeping Granville as a summer
retreat. As disappointing as it was to leave
behind the magic of the house, he was thrilled
to have experienced the final years of the
Belle Époque, before the outbreak of the First
World War. This would inspire his taste in
fashion and his desire to find joy in luxury.

# BOHEMIAN PARIS

Christian's teenage fascination with the bohemian world of artists and cabaret nightclubs was horrifying to his parents, and they encouraged him to study political science. But it was clear his interest lay in art and design. After dropping out of his studies in 1928, his father reluctantly helped him to open an art gallery. Christian and a friend exhibited works by modernist artists such as cubists Georges Braque and Pablo Picasso, and surrealists Salvador Dalí and Jean Cocteau.

# HARD TIMES

Following the Wall Street Crash of 1929, Maurice was forced to sell his company after losing his investments. The family gave up Granville and moved to a farmhouse in Provence. Further tragedy followed when Christian's brother Bernard was struck down with an incurable nervous disease, and his beloved mother died in 1931.

# FIRST SKETCHES

Without the financial support of his family,
Christian was forced to close the gallery and
to find another way to support himself. He
worked as a magazine illustrator and sold
fashion sketches to couture houses including
Schiaparelli, Balenciaga and Paquin. In
1938, he was hired as an assistant to the
designer Robert Piguet. As Dior gained more
experience, Piguet allowed him to design for
three collections, which helped him nurture a
love of elegant simplicity.

# IN SERVICE

When war broke out in September 1939 it was only a matter of time before Christian was called up for military service. After the Germans swept into Paris in June 1940, he was demobilized and joined his family in the South of France. He helped his father and sister Catherine grow much-needed vegetables, which they sold at local markets.

As the couture houses began to reopen, Dior returned to Paris in 1941. He moved into an apartment on Rue Royale and joined the Lucien Lelong fashion house.

# WARTIME FASHION

Lelong was one of the few designers in Paris who kept working under the occupation, and Dior was forced to design gowns for the wives of collaborators and Nazi officers. Lelong was president of the Chambre Syndicale de la Haute Couture, and he believed keeping fashion going was vital for employment and for the future of the textiles industry.

## CATHERINE DIOR

Dior's youngest sister, Catherine, joined the French Resistance during the war, and would host underground resistance meetings in the Rue Royale apartment. She was captured by the Gestapo in 1944, and after being questioned and tortured, she was sent to Germany on one of the last deportation trains out of France. Catherine was interred at different concentration camps, including the brutal Ravensbrück, where she was forced to do hard labour in inhumane conditions.

With the Allies getting closer, prisoners were sent on a death march to Dresden, but Catherine escaped and made it back to Paris in May 1945. She was so thin and malnourished that her brother didn't recognize her at first. Catherine refused to be broken by her experience, and she testified against the Gestapo to the War Crimes Commission in 1952.

She received numerous awards for her bravery, including the Legion of Honour and the Croix de Guerre. Catherine, however, preferred a life out of the spotlight, and retreated to Provence, selling the flowers she grew in the garden.

# LIBERATION

While Christian Dior worked under the constraints of rationing to design wartime fashions, he disliked Parisian street style, which he described as "hideous". Women followed a "zazou" fashion for boxy jackets, short skirts and bulky platform shoes, while their expressive turbans and hats were a way of silently defying the occupying forces.

Paris was liberated by the Allies in 1944, but the city was scarred by damaged buildings, and suffered under rationing and a thriving black market. Now that the war was over, Dior wanted to move beyond the unflattering fashions, to revive the traditions of couture, and to embrace femininity to symbolize recovery.

"Traces of it were all around me – damaged buildings, devastated countryside, rationing, the black market, and less serious, but of more immediate interest to me, hideous fashions. Hats were far too large, skirts far too short, jackets far too long, shoes far too heavy."

CHRISTIAN DIOR,
*DIOR BY DIOR* (1956)

# LUCKY MEETING

In 1946, Dior had a chance encounter on the street with wealthy textile manufacturer Marcel Boussac. He asked Dior if he would be interested in reviving Philippe et Gaston, a brand established in 1922. Instead, Dior chose to do something new. He wanted to create a design house that would bring hope to post-war France and hark back to the country's dressmaking traditions. He envisioned a fashion house that would produce couture for elegant clientele while promoting simplicity and a return to great luxury.

Dior opened the house in December 1946, and his first collection was shown in February 1947.

# "All around us, life was beginning anew: it was time for a new trend in fashion."

CHRISTIAN DIOR,
*DIOR BY DIOR* (1956)

# 30 AVENUE MONTAIGNE

Dior discovered 30 Avenue Montaigne while searching for a home for his workrooms and salon. Situated on a tree-lined street close to the prestigious Hôtel Plaza Athénée and the Théâtre des Champs-Elysées, it was the perfect spot to attract the cream of fashionable society. The salon was decorated in simple white and pearl grey, with crystal chandeliers and potted palms.

When it was first opened, there were three workrooms in the attic, a salon and office space. As business grew, Dior expanded into 32 Avenue Montaigne, and 13 François 1er, which would be home to the Dior boutique when it opened in 1955.

# FIRST COLLECTION

On 12 February 1947 Christian Dior unveiled his first collection. It would be one of the most impactful debuts in fashion history. After years of austerity and fabric rationing, he wanted to embrace the feminine silhouette with corsets, padding and yards of expensive fabric, as if returning to the Belle Époque.

Having found inspiration in the open petals of roses, he named his collection Corolle. He brought an architect's eye to his dressmaking techniques, constructing his clothes as if they were buildings. He melded dresses to the natural curves of the body, and there was a simplicity to his silhouettes, with fluid, clean lines.

# A NEW LOOK

Dior kept the designs secret until the day of the show and huge crowds gathered outside his salon in anticipation. *Harper's Bazaar* editor Carmel Snow was so enthusiastic that she called it a "New Look", and the name caught on (see page 8). It was so well-received that Dior became famous overnight. Coco Chanel, however, wasn't impressed. "Dior doesn't dress women, he upholsters them", she said.

## TOILES

As he collected his ideas, Dior scribbled down preliminary sketches, known as the "petites gravures". Once finalized, these would be passed to the premières who took responsibility for different sketches. The premières draped muslin fabric around a dress dummy, shaping and pinning it to match the sketch. These would be known as the "toiles".

Dior viewed these first toiles several times until deciding which would make the final cut. He then selected the fabric, buttons, belts and jewels for each dress. Rather than choosing a fabric for its colour, he selected it for its texture, and how it would perform on the body. After showing the collection, clients would reserve the pieces they wanted to purchase. Every gown was made to measure, and the customer was required to come in for many fittings until it was perfect.

# AMERICAN ACCOLADES

Dior courted the wealthiest customers who could afford his luxury couture. His most devoted clients were in the United States, and in September 1947 he was invited to Dallas, Texas, by department store Neiman Marcus. He was presented with their fashion award, becoming the first French designer to receive it.

Following success in the States, Dior opened an atelier in New York in 1948. Christian Dior–New York was located on the corner of Fifth Avenue and 57th Street.

# CARACAS DRESS

Success in the United States was followed by
the opening of Dior's first South American
store in Caracas, Venezuela, in 1953. It was
a replica of his Avenue Montaigne salon and
was operated by staff who had been trained
in Paris. His presence in the city inspired him
to design the black silk faille off-the-shoulder
Caracas dress, for the Spring/Summer 1957
collection, which was worn by Sophia Loren.

"I designed clothes for flower-like women, with rounded shoulders, full feminine busts, and hand-span waists above enormous spreading skirts."

CHRISTIAN DIOR,
*DIOR BY DIOR* (1956)

# OVER THE TOP

At a time when Parisians were still living in hardship as the city recovered from war, Dior's excessive use of fabric was aggravating to many people. When Dior held a photoshoot at Lepic market in Montmartre, a group of female stallholders were so incensed at the extravagance, they physically attacked a model, trying to rip the dress from her body. The anger also crossed the Channel. With fabric rationing still in place in Britain, MP Mabel Ridealgh called it "a stupidly exaggerated use of material".

# ROYAL LINKS

Dior loved English traditions and culture. He admired country house architecture and English gardens like the one cultivated by his mother at Granville. In 1950 Dior hosted his first London show at the Savoy Hotel in London. There was such a huge demand for tickets that the collection was held over three sittings.

While in London, he also made a discreet trip to the French Embassy, where he presented a private fashion show to Queen Elizabeth (later the Queen Mother) and her daughter Princess Margaret.

# LONDON STORE

Christian Dior London opened in 1952, and he held another show in 1954 at Blenheim Palace, to raise money for the Red Cross. Organized by the Duchess of Marlborough and attended by Princess Margaret, it established him as the French couturier to the aristocracy.

# FOLLOWING THE LINE

Dior chose themes for his collections, which included naming a series of gowns after musicians, authors and flowers. There was the Tulip line for Spring/Summer 1953, and the Lily-of-the-valley line the following year. By the mid-1950s he was using letters to represent the shape of his collections.

Following on from the H line for Autumn/ Winter 1954, Dior introduced the A line, which loosened the silhouette and flared at the hips. He considered the letter "A" a perfect representation of the shape of the collection, with variations on the silhouette for day and for night. The letter "Y" was given to his Autumn/Winter 1955 collection as the dresses featured full skirts, inverted Y-shaped pleats and deep V-necks.

# TRAGIC DEATH

Dior appeared on the cover of *Time* magazine in March 1957 wielding a pair of scissors, but only a few months later he was dead. He was on holiday in Montecatini, Italy, when he was struck down by a fatal heart attack on 24 October 1957.

The fashion world was in shock at the news. Two and a half thousand people attended his funeral, and among the crowd of mourners was his successor, Yves Saint Laurent.

# CHAPTER TWO

# CLOTHING & COLLECTIONS

DIOR

# PURE EXTRAVAGANCE

When the New Look was shown in 1947, it revolutionized French couture. Defined by its cinched waist, round shoulders, accentuated hips and full petticoats under calf-length skirts, it was an extravagant and feminine alternative to wartime uniforms.

# RAISING THE BAR

There were 95 looks with two silhouettes –
the Corolle, with full skirts like the petals of
flowers, and the En Huit, with its streamlined
pencil skirts. The most iconic design was the
Bar suit, with its tailored, nipped-in ivory
jacket that rounded at the hips, and black
pleated, ballet-length skirt made from 13 feet
(4 metres) of wool. As the symbol of Dior, it
has been reinterpreted and adapted by every
creative director since.

# ZIG ZAGGING

Named for the asymmetry of his gowns, Dior's Zig Zag collection for Autumn/Winter 1948 further built on the New Look triumph with an architect's eye for structure and proportion. The "winged" gowns achieved movement through a deep inverted pleat at the back and front of the skirts.

# LOOKING BACK

To fit with the post-war joy in Paris, Dior used ruffle details on his skirts for a fantasy version of historical gowns. The Eugénie ball gown harked back to the 19th-century crinolines of the Empress Eugénie, wife of Napoléon III of France. It featured layers of blush-pink tulle for a tiered cascading skirt, with a sculpted lace bodice. *Women's Wear Daily* described the collection as modern and wearable despite the yards of fabric and extravagant embroidery.

## MILIEU DU SIÈCLE

For his Autumn/Winter 1949 collection,
Dior created two of his most sought designs,
Venus and Junon, both named after Roman
goddesses. They confirmed his reputation
as a designer weaving fantasies. Venus,
in his signature grey, featured cascading
tears decorated with iridescent beading and
embroidery for a feathered effect. Junon was
a strapless gown with a skirt constructed from
iridescent blue-green petals. It was designed
to appear like the feathers of a peacock, and
the sequin-embroidered tulle was crafted by
master embroiderer Rébé.

# IN PROFILE

The grey silk Cigale gown with its structured bodice, was one of the most iconic dresses from the Autumn/Winter 1952 Profile line, which featured angles and sharp silhouettes.

Praised by *Vogue* as a masterpiece of construction, the boned corset pushed up the breasts, cinched in the waist, and pushed the hips forward, like scaffolding around the body.

Another success from the same collection was the Palmyre gown, purchased by the Duchess of Windsor. Pale blue satin was embroidered with lamé thread flowers, pearls, sequins and rhinestones.

# YVES SAINT LAURENT

Yves Saint Laurent was an 18-year-old student designer who had only been in Paris for a short time when he began working for Christian Dior. Three years later, in 1958, he was appointed Dior's successor as per the late designer's wishes.

Born in Algeria, Saint Laurent moved to Paris in 1954, having won third prize in a prestigious fashion competition held by the International Wool Secretariat. Under Dior's tutelage, Saint Laurent learned the skills of haute couture. Dior called him an "immense talent", and he trusted him enough to allow him to contribute his designs and share the glory.

# DEBUT SHOW

Saint Laurent's debut show for Dior was shown on 30 January 1958, and it caused much excitement. The Trapèze collection was considered so refreshing that he received a standing ovation. To appeal to a hip, young audience he reinvented the New look by combining the full skirt with the loose frocks of the 1920s. There were cocktail dresses, evening gowns, mohair afternoon dresses and coats in this new, waistless silhouette, and the breezy style appealed to those looking for something fresh and youthful. The L'Eléphant Blanc dress was a variation of the Trapèze shape, with a corseted understructure hidden by the loose, rhinestone-decorated tulle outer layer.

# FINAL SHOW

Over the next two years, Saint Laurent designed six collections for Dior. He wanted to create youthful fashions for a new generation. Saint Laurent's final collection for Dior, Souplesse, Légèreté, Vie, was a beatnik tribute, comprising blacks and purples, crocodile-style leather and turtlenecks, but it wasn't well received. One of the key pieces was the Chicago jacket, a luxury adaption of the leather motorcycle jacket, with black crocodile skin and a mink trim.

# MOVING ON

Following the outbreak of the Algerian War, Saint Laurent was drafted for military duty in September 1960. Training proved so traumatic that after 20 days he suffered a mental breakdown and was hospitalized. He was eventually replaced by the more traditional Marc Bohan. Once Saint Laurent recovered, he launched his own company, which would go on to make its own fashion history.

# MARC BOHAN

Marc Bohan understood that the house relied on its wealthy, more conservative clients. Following his appointment in 1961, his functional couture appealed to society figures and actresses like Elizabeth Taylor and Grace Kelly. Over his 30 years as creative director, Bohan fitted with the brand rather than letting his personality take over. He even chose to wear the cotton smocks that Dior had favoured while designing in his workrooms.

Born Roger Maurice Louis Bohan in Paris in 1926 to a milliner mother, he initially studied finance, but like Dior, he chose to pursue fashion. In 1945 he trained with Dior's mentor Robert Piguet. After four years there, he worked as an assistant to Edward Molyneux, and was then hired in 1954 to lead the traditional Paris fashion house Jean Patou. He arrived at Dior in 1958, where he was tasked with designing the London line, until he succeeded Yves Saint Laurent as chief designer and artistic director.

"I don't have any high philosophy about fashion. My attitude is very simple. We must always give women something new, something unexpected."

MARC BOHAN,
*SUNDAY DISPATCH*, 9 OCTOBER 1960

# SLIM LOOK

Bohan's debut Spring/Summer collection for Dior, shown in January 1961, was inspired by the 1920s with its knee-length dresses and slim suits. It was declared a "smash hit" by Carrie Donovan, the fashion editor of the *New York Times Magazine*. She described the enthusiastic crowd clapping, cheering, toppling chairs and smashing champagne glasses. Elizabeth Taylor put in an order for a dozen dresses, and Marlene Dietrich snapped up a suit. Bohan believed elegance didn't need to be showy and chose to design simple but luxurious couture.

# DR ZHIVAGO

Marc Bohan was inspired by the wintery Russian landscapes and costumes of the 1965 film *Doctor Zhivago* for his Autumn/Winter 1966 collection. He designed leather boots, fur-lined coats and hoods, military greatcoats and soldier's caps for his critically-acclaimed collection. It tapped into the popularity of Julie Christie's look and Phyllis Dalton's costumes for the film, and Bohan's interpretation would be a reference point for other designers.

# OBLIQUE MOTIF

In 1967, Bohan created the Oblique pattern, which he named after Dior's Autumn/ Winter 1950 collection. It wasn't put to use until two years later, for the Spring/Summer 1969 collection when the repetition of the "D" logo appeared on a shoulder bag. It would later be introduced to shoes and other accessories.

"I'm not designing to please myself or for a photograph. I am designing for a woman who wants to look her best. I have always in mind the reaction of women I know."

MARC BOHAN,
*THE NEW YORK TIMES*, 9 SEPTEMBER 2023

# WIDER AUDIENCE

While Bohan's designs were traditional, he was also willing to embrace more youthful lines and to adopt bold colours and patterns to appeal to the "youthquake" generation. In the 1960s, as ready-to-wear became more popular, Dior needed to adjust to these changing demands. The first ready-to-wear line, Miss Dior, was launched in 1967 by Philippe Guibourgé.

Bohan also introduced a children's collection, Baby Dior. Selling matching mother-and-daughter outfits, it was inspired by Elizabeth Taylor's request for Bohan to design for her daughter, Maria Burton. The boutique was officially opened by Grace Kelly in November 1967. Two years later, in 1969, Bohan introduced a menswear line, Christian Dior Monsieur.

# LVMH

In 1984, French investor Bernard Arnault acquired the Boussac group, which gave him control of Christian Dior. To make it more profitable, Arnault wanted to expand on the different lines and accessories, including children's clothing, perfumes and cosmetics. Following further acquisitions, Arnault formed LVMH in 1987, with Christian Dior forming a key part of this global luxury goods company.

# GIANFRANCO FERRÉ

Even though Dior made $650 million in sales in 1988, and Bohan had won the Golden Thimble award in 1983 and 1988, he was dismissed in 1989, and controversially replaced by the Italian designer Gianfranco Ferré. As Dior's artistic director from 1989 to 1996, Ferré chose a more cutting-edge approach. Rather than romance, his designs were about architecture. Over his 15 couture collections for Dior, he played with volume and cutting techniques.

Born in 1944 in Legnano, near Milan, Italy, Ferré studied architecture in Milan, and soon after graduating in 1969, he moved into fashion as an accessories and raincoat designer. He launched his own successful fashion label, Baila, in 1974, which he returned to when he left Dior in 1996.

# ASCOT—CECIL BEATON

For his debut Autumn/Winter collection in 1989, Gianfranco Ferré tapped into Dior's love of the Edwardian era by creating an homage to Cecil Beaton's costumes for the 1964 musical *My Fair Lady*, starring Audrey Hepburn. As well as the feminine Ascot finery of pale silks and organzas, he also introduced the masculine, with hardy tweeds and flannels for frock coats and suits. He also embraced Dior's love of flowers, with floral prints, corsages and ballgown embellishments.

# JOHN GALLIANO

John Galliano's experimental eye shook up the brand when he was appointed in 1997. He brought flamboyance and theatrics to his shows, while also introducing cult items like the Saddle bag, the newspaper print dress and the "J'adore Dior" T-shirt.

Gibraltar-born Galliano made a name for himself after graduating from Central Saint Martins art school, London, with a New Romantic-inspired collection in 1984. He was appointed as head designer of Givenchy in 1995 before switching to Dior. At a time when Alexander McQueen and Marc Jacobs were shaking up fashion, Galliano's rebelliousness was an asset. He also counted Naomi Campbell and Kate Moss as two of his most loyal model supporters.

# CLOCHARDS

John Galliano first introduced the iconic newspaper print in his controversial Spring/Summer 2000 couture collection, dubbed "homeless chic". He was inspired by the rough sleepers on the banks of the Seine on his way to work each morning. He printed press clippings from the *International Herald Tribune* onto fabric, which included reviews of previous collections.

The theme was continued in the Autumn/Winter 2000 collection, with an invented newspaper, *The Christian Dior Daily*, printed onto chiffons, leathers, and the reverse side of furs.

# SHAKING THINGS UP

Galliano plundered history, opera and pop culture for his influences, ranging from Napoleon, presented as a glam rock star, to Versailles. There was the *Matrix* look of Autumn/Winter 1999, the gold pharaohs of his Spring/Summer 2004 collection, and the flamenco dancers for his Autumn/Winter 2003 dance-themed show, which was also a tribute to his Spanish father. Controversial in both his collections and his personal life, Galliano left Dior in 2011.

# RAF SIMONS

Following Galliano's dismissal, the Belgian designer Raf Simons became head designer in 2012. Over the next three years, the Belgian designer stayed true to the elegant luxury of Dior. He used intricate embroidery and beading on minimalist, wasp-waist silhouettes, while also experimenting with latex catsuits and duchesse satin trousers.

Simons helped boost the brand by securing Rihanna as the brand's first Black ambassador, and as he introduced popular items such as couture trainers, sales soon increased by 60 per cent.

"Dior's ultimate obsession is that he wanted them to wear it. I want them to wear it in the street. If it doesn't relate to the outside then it would be very theatrical for me."

RAF SIMONS,
*VOGUE*, 23 OCTOBER 2015

## CLASSIC STYLE

For his Autumn/Winter 2012 debut collection, Raf Simons moved away from Galliano's maximalism to create simple lines that harked back to the classic style of Dior. Drawn to the founder's love of the countryside, he used flowers as a symbol of rebirth with his embroidered and appliquéd floral bodices and delicate net gloves. There were also simple monochrome designs, with Jennifer Lawrence wearing a strapless cream gown from the collection when she picked up her first Oscar in 2013.

# MARIA GRAZIA CHIURI

Maria Grazia Chiuri gave Dior a feminist makeover when she was named artistic director in 2016. As the first woman to lead the house, she wanted to update it for a new generation. Chiuri, originally from Rome, was working as co-creative director for Valentino when she was offered the role.

She showcased buzzy slogan T-shirts such as "We should all be feminists" and "C'est non non non et non!" ("It's no, no, no, and no!"). She was committed to the heritage, creating traditional luxury such as a tulle "Dior red" ball gown. But she also wanted to make it more practical, with T-shirts, denim and sneakers. Some of Chiuri's key pieces included ribbon slingback flats, updated Saddle bags, and the revived Bar jacket.

# FEMININE CONCEPTS

In her Spring/Summer 2020 couture collection, Maria Grazia Chiuri collaborated with American artist Judy Chicago for a glittering feminist concept based on the artist's installation, *The Dinner Party*. She also partnered with Chanakya, the Mumbai-based embroidery house, to support their School of Craft, which trains women from low-income backgrounds. The show, held in a symbolic womb, envisioned a world where women were in charge.

# ART MEETS FASHION

One of Chiuri's strengths was merging art with fashion, calling attention to the artisans who don't normally get recognition. She consistently worked with female artists and photographers, and during the pandemic, Chiuri showed her Resort collection in Italy to support her home country's recovery from the pandemic.

Chiuri also celebrated the work of Chanakya in a multi-coloured pre-fall 2023 collection at the Gateway of India, Mumbai, which embraced the skilled craftspeople and traditions of India.

*Miss Dior*

EAU DE PARFUM

#WAKEUPFORLOVE

**DIOR**

# CHAPTER THREE

# LUXURY
# ACCESSORIES

# A COMPLETE LOOK

Dior wished to provide women with everything they needed to achieve the ultimate in elegance. Hats were vital to the look, with the straw hat appearing as the final flourish to complete the Bar suit.

In 1950, just four years after founding his fashion house, Dior expanded his line to include perfumes, furs and stockings. An accessories boutique was originally located at the bottom of the staircase at 30 Avenue Montaigne. It sold jewels, flowers, scarves and simplified dresses based on the collection. In 1955, a new boutique opened on the corner of Avenue Montaigne and Rue François 1er, to sell perfumes and makeup.

"Personally I consider that a woman without a hat is not completely dressed."

CHRISTIAN DIOR,
*DIOR BY DIOR* (1956)

"A woman's perfume tells more about her than her handwriting."

CHRISTIAN DIOR,
PAIRFUM.COM, 2024

# FIRST FRAGRANCE

In March 1947, Dior formed a perfume company, Christian Dior Parfums, which was overseen by his childhood friend, Serge Heftler-Louiche.

The first perfume, Miss Dior, was released in December of that year. Created by perfumier Paul Vacher, it was named in honour of his sister Catherine. Dior sprayed his salon with the floral scent as he prepared to unveil his first collection.

"Dior has always been committed to women and luxury. Being led by women makes it a real celebration and encouragement of women and women artists."

NATALIE PORTMAN,
*VOGUE*, MARCH 2024

# THE RIGHT SCENT

Dior worked with master perfumer Edmond
Roudnitska to develop further scents,
including Diorama in 1949, and Diorissimo
in 1956, with its lily-of-the-valley notes.
Roudnitska would continue to develop new
perfumes for Dior until the 1980s.

In 2005, Miss Dior Chérie was launched,
a youthful version of the fragrance with
notes of strawberry and popcorn. It was
reformulated in 2011 and named simply
Miss Dior, with Natalie Portman serving
as its ambassador.

DIOR

# PERFUMERY

Christian Dior's perfumes include:

- Miss Dior (1947)
- Diorama (1949)
- Eau Fraîche (1953)
- Diorissimo (1956)
- Diorling (1963)
- Eau Sauvage, the first Eau de Toilette for men (1966)
- Diorella (1972)
- Dioressence (1979)
- Eau Sauvage Extrême, men's fragrance (1984)
- Poison (1985)

## LUXURY ACCESSORIES

- Fahrenheit, men's fragrance (1988)
- Dune (1991)
- Dolce Vita (1995)
- Dune for men (1997)
- J'adore (1999)
- Dior Addict (2001)
- Higher (2002)
- Pure Poison (2004)
- Miss Dior Chérie (2005)
- Dior Homme (2005)
- Launch of the Christian Dior Collection Privée (2010)
- Hypnotic Poison (2013)

# WHAT'S YOUR POISON?

Poison was a bestseller on its release in 1985, and in 1999 J'adore, created by Calice Becker, became one of the most popular perfumes in the world. Charlize Theron was the face of J'adore for 20 years, until she was replaced by Rihanna in 2024. As the new "queen" of the scent, Rihanna was shot by Steven Klein for the commercial in which she dripped with gold in the majestic surroundings of Versailles.

# SAUVAGE MALE

Dior's first men's fragrance, Eau Sauvage, was released in 1966. It was created by Edmond Roudnitska, who developed a fresh, citrus aroma with top notes including lemon, bergamot and basil. Its name was said to have been inspired by Percy Savage, the Australian publicist. In 2009, New Wave actor Alain Delon was invited to be its ambassador. In an unprecedented move, the campaign used a portrait taken of him as a young man by Jean-Marie Périer, from the same year the fragrance was introduced. With the aura of a charming bad boy, other faces of the scent have included French singer Johnny Hallyday in 2009, and more controversially, Johnny Depp.

## COSMETICS

Parfum Christian Dior first introduced
its range of lipsticks in 1955, coming in
22 different shades. It wasn't until 1969,
however, that a Christian Dior makeup line
was fully developed. It was conceived by Serge
Lutens, who created a bold colour collection,
L'Explosion de Couleurs for Spring/Summer
1969. The first skincare line, Hydra Dior,
was launched in 1973.

# ADDICTION

When Dior Addict perfume was launched in
2002, it was accompanied by a new makeup
range. Lip glosses were a staple of the new
millennium, and the Dior Addict Ultra Gloss was
a cult favourite. It boasted the high pigmentation
of a lipstick, with a sheer, shiny look. Each one
was given a luscious name, such as a "A Craving
for Truffles" or "A Desire for Sweets".

The lip glosses were accompanied by Dior
Addict nail lacquer, which came in a range of
candy shades. The original advertising for Dior
Addict proved to be controversial, particularly
with its tagline "Admit it", which played on
associations with other forms of addiction.

## ICONIC PIECES

In 1953, the Christian Dior–Delman company was set up to sell shoes created by Roger Vivier. These embellished beauties were wrapped in off-cuts of the fabrics from the gowns, including Impressionist floral prints, or decorated with flowers, such as lily-of-the-valley.

Dior accessorized his New Look gowns with satin clutches and leather satchels, but it wasn't until the 1990s that the It bag would reign.

Dior

# THE LADY DIOR BAG

Dreamed up by Gianfranco Ferré in 1995, the Lady Dior bag, originally called Chouchou, was renamed for its famous devotee, Princess Diana. In 1995, Bernadette Chirac, wife of French president Jacques Chirac, asked Dior to custom make a bag to gift to Princess Diana. The black, quilted leather, box-shaped bag was said to be inspired by the chairs that Dior used in his salon. It would also be adapted in different sizes and materials for further collections.

# THE SADDLE BAG

John Galliano's Saddle bag was a nod to the equestrian world, with its saddle shape and "D"-shaped stirrup charm. It first appeared in the Spring/Summer 2000 ready-to-wear show, slung over the shoulder of models in denim and over-the-knee boots. Carrie Bradshaw in *Sex and the City* adored hers, and in the early noughties it was the It bag for It girls like Paris Hilton and Nicole Richie. Maria Grazia Chiuri brought back the bag for her Americana patchwork collection for Autumn/Winter 2018.

# DIORAMA BAG

The Diorama bag was Raf Simons' contribution to the history of Dior, updated for the modern woman. Named after the 1948 perfume, the cult bag was introduced in 2015, and was created as a tribute to actress Marion Cotillard. It had a vintage feel, with its simple design featuring a classic flap, a chain strap and discreet branding. Its leather or suede fabric was embellished with cutting-edge laser techniques, precision stitching and embossing.

# THE BOOK TOTE

For Spring/Summer 2018, Maria Grazia Chiuri
introduced the Book tote, an easy canvas bag
with two top handles, which was based on
a 1967 sketch by Marc Bohan. Available in a
variety of sizes and patterns, including floral
and Dior Oblique logo embroidery, it was
perfect for lugging around a favourite book.

# SLOGAN T-SHIRTS

John Galliano introduced the cult "J'adore Dior"
T-shirt on the Spring/Summer 2001 runway.
Simple, accessible and fun, it was an easy way
for someone to tap into their appreciation of
the brand. Decades later, models Bella Hadid
and Kendall Jenner picked up vintage tees to
reference the nostalgia for Y2K fashion.

## LUXURY ACCESSORIES

The "We Should All Be Feminists" T-shirt
was the star of Maria Grazia Chiuri's debut
collection for Spring/Summer 2017. As the first
female creative director, she delivered a strong
message by teaming the slogan, taken from
Nigerian author Chimamanda Ngozi Adichie's
groundbreaking essay from 2014, with sheer
tulle ballet skirts. The T-shirts were a hit on
Instagram and among feminist-leaning
celebrities. Proceeds from the sale of the
T-shirt went to the Clara Lionel Foundation,
Rihanna's non-profit organization.

CHAPTER FOUR

# PEOPLE & POP CULTURE

# DEVOTED CLIENTELE

From the moment he opened the doors of his salon, Dior attracted a glamorous clientele. As well as wealthy Parisian society ladies, his customers included British aristocracy and Hollywood royalty. Marc Bohan further established Dior as the go-to label for dazzling couture, as worn by Sophia Loren, Lauren Bacall and Grace Kelly. He even designed an extravagant embroidered velvet gown for the 1967 coronation of the Iranian empress Farah Pahlavi.

Under more recent creative directors, devotees include Kate Moss, Jennifer Lawrence and Bella Hadid, while Natalie Portman and Rihanna have been long-standing ambassadors.

# "When I first saw the dress on the runway, I fell in love. Polka dots are classic and chic."

JENNIFER LAWRENCE,
*VOGUE*, 10 MARCH 2024

## DIOR ON FILM

In Christian Dior's memoirs, he noted that the first film he worked on was 1939's *School for Scandal*, after being asked by actor Marcel Herrand to make the costumes. By the time of his first fashion show, he had designed for eight films. The early films featuring Dior's designs are:

♦ *School for Scandal* (1939)

♦ *Le lit à colonnes* (1942)

♦ *Lettres d'amour* (1942)

♦ *Le Baron fantôme* (1943)

- ◆ *Les Roquevillard* (1943)
- ◆ *Paméla* (1945)
- ◆ *Échec au roy* (1945)
- ◆ *Sylvie et le fantôme* (1946)
- ◆ *Pour une nuit d'amour* (1947)
- ◆ *Man About Town* (1947)
- ◆ *Les Enfants Terribles* (1949)
- ◆ *Sous le ciel de Paris* (1951)

# LEADING LADIES

Once Dior was a household name, he was hired to design for an increasing number of movies, and was also sought after by top actresses to create their costumes. After designing for *Stage Fright* (1950), Dior also costumed Marlene Dietrich in *No Highway in the Sky* (1951). He also designed Ava Gardner's costumes in *The Little Hut* (1957) and Olivia de Havilland's entire wardrobe for *The Ambassador's Daughter* (1956).

# RITA HAYWORTH

Rita Hayworth purchased several pieces from Dior's debut collection, including a black "daffodil stem" dress. For the Paris premiere of *Gilda* in 1947, she chose an organza tiered evening gown. As a dedicated client throughout the 1950s, Rita was pictured wearing sunglasses on the front row of the 1956 salon show.

# MARLENE DIETRICH

Before agreeing to star in Alfred Hitchcock's *Stage Fright* (1950) Marlene Dietrich insisted that Christian Dior design her screen wardrobe. "No Dior, No Dietrich", she famously told the director, and Dior created a lavish wardrobe of extravagant gowns that used yards of tulle and feathers. Dior also dressed Dietrich in a black cocktail dress for the 1951 Academy Awards, calculating the vertical slit in the skirt to match the angle from which she would access the stage. The film and cabaret star was so devoted to Dior that she moved into an apartment on Avenue Montaigne to be closer to the salon.

# ELIZABETH TAYLOR

Edith Head was indebted to the New Look when she designed costumes for Elizabeth Taylor in *A Place in the Sun* (1951). The white strapless gown with its frothy embroidered skirt became the most requested prom dress that year.

Taylor wore the Soirée à Rio dress when she collected her Oscar for Best Actress for *Butterfield 8* in 1961. From the Spring/Summer 1961 collection, it featured a yellow bodice, a white bubble skirt covered in embroidered flowers and a red rose on a green belt. Taylor considered it her good luck charm and would continue to wear similar styles. This "Oscar" dress was thought lost for many years until it was discovered in an old suitcase in London.

## GRACE KELLY

As Princess Grace of Monaco, the former
Hollywood star was an adored client of Dior,
with a third of her wardrobe consisting of Dior
outfits. Marc Bohan was so close to Princess
Grace, that he acted as a beloved uncle to her
daughters, and designed Caroline of Monaco's
wedding gown. They had a deep friendship
and a shared love of elegance, and she also
embraced more daring looks. She wore a
colourful, boho-style dress at a gala dinner in
Monaco in 1968. It tapped into the hippie-chic
trend, and was such a favourite that she wore it
several times.

## MARILYN MONROE

Marilyn Monroe wore a black backless Dior gown for *Vogue* magazine in 1962, in what became known as the "Last Sitting". Photographer Bert Stern arrived at the Hotel Bel Air to take a second series of images of Marilyn for the magazine, after she wore just a bed sheet for the first. He named the photo *Looking Over Shoulder*, and it demonstrated her poise and confidence when wearing haute couture.

# PRINCESS MARGARET

For Princess Margaret's twenty-first birthday in 1951, she ordered a Dior gown from the Oblique collection, which she also wore in her official portrait by Cecil Beaton. Dior described her as a "real fairytale princess: delicate, graceful, exquisite", and he wrapped her in an off-the-shoulder silk organza layered gown, scattered with mother-of-pearl and beading.

# MARGOT FONTEYN

Prima ballerina Margot Fonteyn often visited the salon, and Dior created the H line wedding gown for her 1955 nuptials to Roberto Arias, the Panamanian ambassador to London. She also ordered the strapless grey silk gown, Soirée de Decembre, from the Autumn/Winter 1955 collection. The front of the skirt was shorter, at calf length, while the back of the skirt featured a train that swept the floor.

# JULIETTE GRÉCO

While he was designing for wealthy, established clients, young women were also enthusiastic about Dior. Juliette Gréco, the existentialist singer who dressed in black, was drawn to the New Look as a youthful style for the future.

"Juliette Gréco understood how to conciliate the demands of her own individual style with those of my designs. Thus the New Look became symbolic of youth and the future."

CHRISTIAN DIOR,
*DIOR BY DIOR* (1956)

# BIANCA JAGGER

From her showstopping moments at Studio 54, to her 1971 wedding to Mick Jagger and nights out with David Bowie, Bianca Jagger was synonymous with 1970s style. The Nicaraguan socialite was also a common presence on the front row of Marc Bohan's Dior shows. She wore a pale pink layered gown to Loulou de la Falaise's wedding in 1977, which she described as "one of the most beautiful and feminine dresses I have ever had."

# PRICE OF FASHION

After filing for divorce from Mick Jagger in 1979, she asked for financial support, which included payment of her clothing bills to Dior and Yves Saint Laurent. Bianca continues to be a fan of Dior under Maria Grazia Chiuri's reign, admiring her feminist stance and her concern for the environmental impact of fashion.

"Marc Bohan was a great Couturier. He was also a lovely man, modest, unpretentious, he always listened to you. He left an incalculable legacy for Maison Dior."

BIANCA JAGGER,
*TATLER*, 20 SEPTEMBER 2023

# PRINCESS DIANA

On 9 December 1996, Princess Diana arrived at the Metropolitan Museum of Art in New York, to attend the Christian Dior-themed Gala and exhibition. She chose a midnight blue silk slip dress by John Galliano, which had featured in his first collection for Dior.

The black lace trim and matching robe was a world apart from the gowns she wore as a member of the royal family. It was so daring, she had second thoughts as to whether it might cause embarrassment to her sons. Following her recent divorce, the dress was a dazzling reminder that she had entered a new chapter in her life, of independence and freedom. This would also be her one and only Met Gala.

# NICOLE KIDMAN

For the 1997 Oscars, Nicole Kidman selected a chartreuse chinoiserie gown from John Galliano's Spring/Summer 1997 couture collection. The absinthe-hued silk slip of a dress, with a slit at the side and delicate floral embroidery, was a statement about Galliano's arrival in Hollywood. Kidman was credited with bringing haute couture to the red carpet.

# CHARLIZE THERON

As the face of J'adore perfume from 2004–24, Charlize Theron wore a series of stunning gold gowns in the advertising campaigns to represent the gilded luxury of the brand. John Galliano designed a gold Swarovski crystal-encrusted gown for the 2008 campaign. It was displayed at the Victoria and Albert Museum in London as part of their 2019 Designer of Dreams exhibition.

Theron wore another exquisite gold gown while hosting the Africa Outreach Project Fundraiser in 2019. The minidress took Dior 1,200 hours to create, as white gauze was painstakingly embellished with gold leather embroidery and a fringed skirt.

# MARION COTILLARD

At the 2009 Academy Awards Marion Cotillard wore a belted tulle couture gown with strips of blue sequins. It was a fitting choice for the actress who starred as a femme fatale in a short film, *The Lady Noire Affair*, to promote the Lady Dior bag that same year.

# JENNIFER LAWRENCE

Actress Jennifer Lawrence has a longstanding relationship with Dior, after being signed as an ambassador in 2012. She made headlines in 2013 when she tripped in her strapless Dior gown while collecting her Oscar for *Silver Linings Playbook*. Since then, Dior has been a mainstay of her red carpet looks.

There was a red strapless gown for the 2014 Oscars, a shimmering pleated halterneck at the European premiere of *Red Sparrow* in 2018, and at the 2018 Oscars she made a powerful statement in a shimmering gown that resembled protective chainmail. She also wore a hand-beaded champagne sheath dress with pleated cape sleeves to showcase her pregnancy bump for the first time at the *Don't Look Up* premiere in New York, in 2022. When she returned to the 2024 Academy Awards, she chose a strapless black gown with white polka dots and matching stole, from the Spring/Summer 2024 haute couture collection.

# SEX AND THE CITY

*Sex and the City*'s costume designer Patricia Field frequently chose Dior for Sarah Jessica Parker and her co-stars. There was the newspaper print dress, the Dior Saddle bag, Dior Logomania knuckleduster rings and gladiator sandals. Lucy Liu also made a guest appearance wearing a "J'adore Dior" T-shirt.

# MRS HARRIS

*Mrs Harris Goes to Paris* (2022) is a historical comedy drama set in 1950s London, and is all about the enticing power of a Dior gown. Mrs Harris, played by Lesley Manville, on seeing a version of the 1957 Caracas dress, feels so in love with it that she would love nothing more than to own one herself. After receiving money from her late husband, she travels to Paris to visit the Dior salon.

# NATALIE PORTMAN

Natalie Portman has been the face of Miss Dior since 2011, and to celebrate the floral scent, she often chooses flower-power Dior gowns for the red carpet. At the 2024 Golden Globes, Portman's couture ball gown was inspired by Impressionist paintings. It featured delicate micro-flower embroidery by the Chanakya School of Craft in Mumbai.

Portman is known to appreciate the feminist statements of Maria Grazia Chiuri's designs. At the 2020 Oscars, she wore a custom-made, black and gold floor-length dress with a black cape, embroidered with the names of female directors who had not been recognized at the awards.

At the 2023 Cannes Film Festival, Portman wore a recreation of the Junon gown to the premiere of her film, *May December*.

## MUSICAL DIOR

As one of the most famous fashion brands, Dior is referenced in the lyrics of songs in many different genres. Here are just a few:

♦ 'Rainbow High' (1996) by Madonna, from *Evita* by Andrew Lloyd Webber

♦ 'Spoiled' (2006) by Pop Smoke (feat. Pharrell Williams)

♦ 'Dance 4 Me' (2009) by Prince

♦ 'Strong Enough' (2009) by 50 Cent

- 'But I am a Good Girl' (2010) by Christina Aguilera, from *Burlesque*

- 'Fashion Killa (2013) by A$AP Rocky

- 'A No No' (2018) by Maria Carey

- 'Dior' (2019) by Pop Smoke

- 'Mamacita' (2020) by Black Eye Peas and Ozuna

- 'Aye' (2023) by Lil Uzi Vert (feat. Travis Scott)

# RIHANNA

Named as the face of J'adore fragrance in 2024, Rihanna has had a longstanding connection to Dior. Under Raf Simons, she became the first Black celebrity to be named ambassador. As well as featuring in their campaigns, she owned the front row, and frequently embraced Dior pink.

When heavily pregnant with her first child in March 2022, Rihanna wore a sheer black negligee to the Paris Dior show, demonstrating how to do maternity wear in style. Returning to Paris Fashion Week for Spring/Summer 2024, Rihanna wore an exaggerated version of the iconic Bar jacket and midi-skirt, accessorized with a Lady Dior bag.

"Everything
I know, see
or hear, every
part of my life is
transformed into
dresses. They are
my daydreams…"

CHRISTIAN DIOR,
*DIOR BY DIOR* (1956)